Progress with Oxford

Numbers and Data Handling

Age 9-10

Hello! I'm Primer and this is Cal.

Contents

OXFORD
UNIVERSITY PRESS

Value your digits

1 Write the value of the shaded digit.

a 9 **3** 4 3

3 hundreds (300)

b 2**7** 5 8 6

c **4**0 7 9 1

d 8 8 **0** 1 2

e 1**1**6 3 4 7

f 5 3**8** 0 3 9

g **7** 7 8 8 0 8

h 8 **2** 5 7 8 5

i **9** 9 3 2 1 4

2 Write each number as the sum of its place values.

Say each number before you write its place values.

a 8 376 = __8__ thousands + __3__ hundreds

+ __7__ tens + __6__ ones

b 28 926 = ____ ten thousands + ____ thousands

+ ____ hundreds + ____ tens + ____ ones

c 31 374 = ____ ten thousands + ____ thousands

+ ____ hundreds + ____ tens + ____ ones

d 484 473 = ____ hundred thousands + ____ ten thousands

+ ____ thousands + ____ hundreds + ____ tens + ____ ones

3 Write the numbers that Cal is describing.

My number has 7 tens,
6 thousands, 3 ones,
8 ten thousands
and 1 hundred.

My number has 6
ones, 9 thousands, 4
hundreds, 5 tens and
9 ten thousands.

a The number is _____. **b** The number is _____.

My number has
2 hundreds, 7 thousands,
3 ones, 4 hundred
thousands, 6 tens and
1 ten thousand.

My number has 4 ten
thousands, 6 thousands,
8 ones and 8 hundred
thousands.

c The number is _____. **d** The number is _____.

---

4 Complete the missing numbers.

a 45672 = __40000__ + 5000 + __600__ + 70 + __2__

b 8__2__7 = _____ + 1000 + _____ + 60 + ____

c _____77 = 90 000 + 9000 + 100 + ____ + ____

d 4____7__3 = _____ + 40 000 + 7000 + _____ + 20 + ____

e __2__8__ = 60 000 + _____ + 500 + ____ + 3

f __0__0____ = 100 000 + 2000 + 70 + 2

Well done!

Give
yourself
a sticker

Check
Make sure you have written the digits in the correct order: thousands
on the left, then hundreds, then tens and then ones on the right. ☐

Now – track how you're doing on page 32!

Talking digits

1 Write the population of each country in words.

> **Remember**
> To read a six-digit number, read the first three digits the way you would read a three-digit number. Then add the word "thousand," and then read the rest of the number. For example, 314 278 is read three hundred and fourteen thousand, two hundred and seventy-eight.

Country	Flag	Population in 2019 (numeral)	Population (words)
a Channel Islands		166 828	one hundred and sixty-six thousand, eight hundred and twenty-eight.
b Iceland		341 566	
c Malta		433 217	
d Luxembourg		596 992	
e Guyana		786 508	
f Fiji		919 070	

2 Match the bags of money.

Some of the numbers sound similar – be careful!

Four hundred and sixty-seven thousand, seven hundred and sixty-four pounds

£476,476   a _____

Six hundred and forty-six thousand, six hundred and forty-seven pounds

£477,646   b _____

Four hundred and seventy-six thousand, four hundred and seventy-six pounds

£674,464   c _____

Six hundred and seventy-four thousand, four hundred and sixty-four pounds

£467,764   d _____

Four hundred and seventy-seven pounds, six hundred and forty-six pounds

£646,647   e _____

3 Add £202 121 to each numeral amount in question 2 and write the new number beside them.

Give yourself a sticker

Check

Check addition by partitioning, e.g. adding 202 121 to a number is the same as adding 200 000 + 2000 + 100 + 20 + 1. ☐

Now – track how you're doing on page 32!

Name that numeral

1 Write each map distance as a numeral.

Remember

Use a space as a thousands separator after every three digits in a number, counting from right to left, e.g. 436 278. We use a hyphen when writing numbers from **twenty-one** to **ninety-nine**.

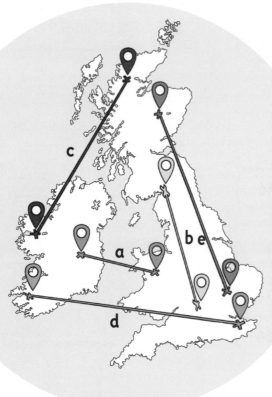

Route	Distance in words (metres)	Distance as a numeral
a	Three hundred and thirty-two thousand, five hundred and fifty-nine metres	
b	Five hundred and eighty-three thousand, one hundred and seventy-four metres	
c	Six hundred and two thousand, three hundred and nineteen metres	
d	Eight hundred thousand, four hundred and seven metres	
e	Nine hundred and eleven thousand, two hundred and twelve metres	

2 Complete the missing digits and words.

	Number in words	Numeral
a	Sixty-two thousand, _____ and _____ -eight	6 ___ 458
b	Three hundred and _____, nine hundred and twenty-one	___ 16 ___ 2 ___
c	_____ thousand, _____ hundred and eighteen	443 ___ ___

3 Write the number words as digits. Then put the numbers in the correct place in the grid.

Across

2 Six hundred and thirteen thousand, nine hundred and ninety-nine _____

3 Nine hundred and seven thousand, five hundred and fifty-five _____

5 Eighty-two thousand, three hundred and forty-six _____

7 Seventy thousand, one hundred and fifteen _____

Down

1 Three hundred and sixty-four thousand, seven hundred and sixteen _____

4 Fifty-four thousand and six _____

6 Two hundred and seventeen thousand, two hundred and eight _____

Check

Say the numeral out loud and check it matches the number in words. ☐

Well done!

Give yourself a sticker

Now – track how you're doing on page 32!

Comparing colonies

Remember

The symbol > means 'greater than', and the symbol < means 'less than'. The arrow always points to the smaller number.

1 Find the correct symbol sticker, **<** or **>** to compare the colonies of ants.

a  43 768 ☐ 43 678

b 79 834 ☐ 79 843

c 91 790 ☐ 91 709

d 643 765 ☐ 643 657

Continue comparing digits left to right to find a place value where the digits differ.

2 Write the symbols **<** or **>** to complete these number statements.

a 12 077 ____ 12 707

b 26 436 ____ 25 364

c 54 589 ____ 54 598

d 263 347 ____ 236 377

e 360 745 ____ 360 475

f 573 424 ____ 573 423

g 666 636 ____ 666 663

h 809 423 ____ 809 422

i 932 828 ____ 932 882

j 986 573 ____ 968 735

Well done!

Give yourself a sticker

Check
Have you used the symbols < and > correctly? ☐

Now – track how you're doing on page 32!

House sales

1 Write the house prices in ascending order.

a

£264 343   £263 344   £264 443   £263 434   £264 334

£_____ < £_____ < £_____ < £_____ < £_____

b

£759 957   £759 759   £795 579   £759 597   £795 499

£_____ < £_____ < £_____ < £_____ < £_____

2 Write the house prices in descending order.

a

£435 367   £453 673   £435 376   £453 637   £435 366

£_____ < £_____ < £_____ < £_____ < £_____

b

£904 540   £904 450   £940 544   £904 504   £940 499

£_____ < £_____ < £_____ < £_____ < £_____

Prices going up!

Give yourself a sticker

Check
Are your answers in the correct order, ascending or descending? ☐

Power up!

1 Count forward in the step size given and write in the numbers that complete the sequence.

a Count forward in 100s.

> 764 >> 864 >> >> >> >> >>

b Count forward in 1000s.

> 18 609 >> 19 609 >> >> >> >> >>

c Count forward in 10 000s.

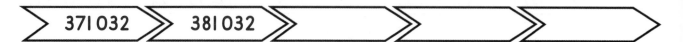

> 371 032 >> 381 032 >> >> >> >>

d Count forward in 100 000s.

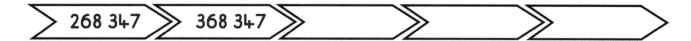

> 268 347 >> 368 347 >> >> >> >>

2 Write in the missing numbers.

a

b

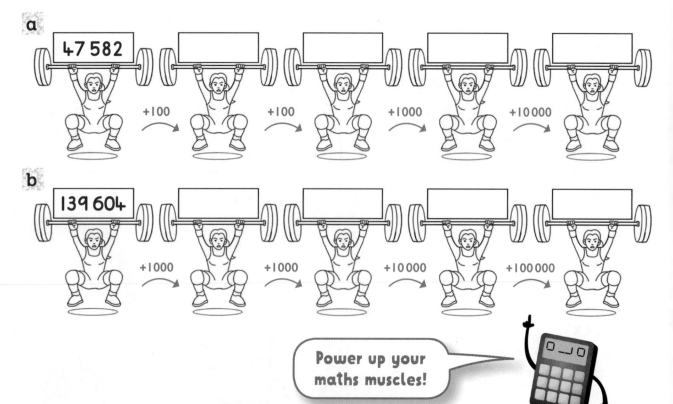

47 582   +100   +100   +1000   +10 000

139 604   +1000   +1000   +10 000   +100 000

Power up your maths muscles!

3 Count backward in the step size given and write in the numbers that complete the sequence.

a Count backward in 100s.

| 917 | 817 | | | | |

b Count backward in 1000s.

| 72 043 | 71 043 | | | | |

c Count backward in 10 000s.

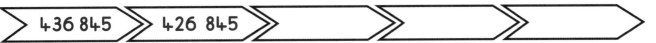

| 436 845 | 426 845 | | | |

d Count backward in 100 000s.

| 956 543 | 856 543 | | | |

4 Write in the missing numbers.

Remember
When a power of ten is added or subtracted only one of the digits should change unless a column boundary is crossed.

a

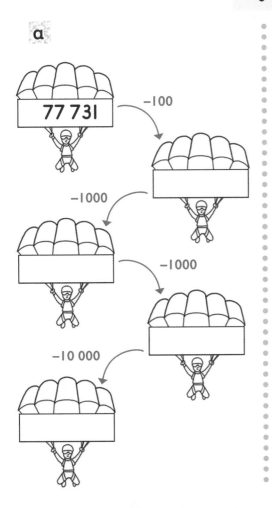

b

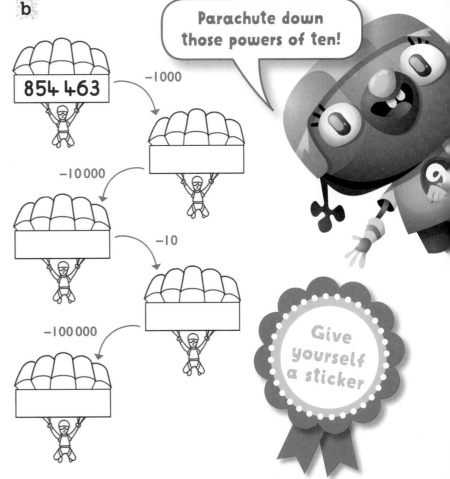

Parachute down those powers of ten!

Give yourself a sticker

Now – track how you're doing on page 32!

Below zero

1 Tick the box that best shows the number.

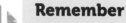

Remember

Negative numbers come before zero on a number line. They are greater the closer they are to zero.

a −37

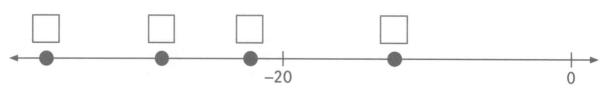

−20   0

b −66

−70   0

c −172

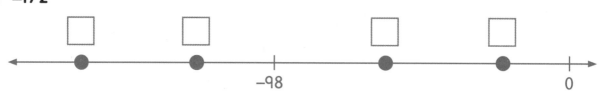

−98   0

2 Circle the thermometer showing the highest temperature.

a

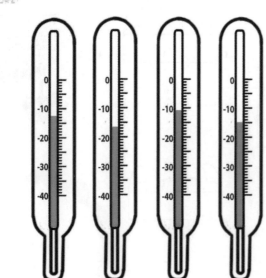

b

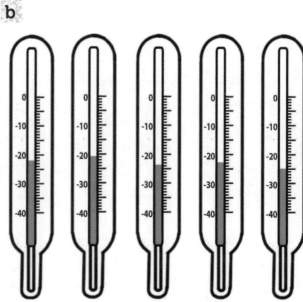

Getting warmer!

3 Write these temperatures in order, the coldest first.

Remember
The greatest number in a sequence of negative numbers is the number closest to zero.

a

 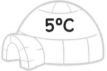   

−3°C   0°C   5°C   3°C   −2°C

_____ _____ _____ _____ _____

b

−21°C   −17°C   −20°C   −19°C   −29°C

_____ _____ _____ _____ _____

c

−38°C   −36°C   −40°C   −39°C   −37°C

_____ _____ _____ _____ _____

4 Use the stickers to complete the number sequences. You won't need all of the stickers.

Negative temperatures means that it is very cold. Brrrrr!

 4°C   1°C    −2°C

 15°C   8°C   1°C

 20°C   11°C   2°C

Give yourself a sticker

Now – track how you're doing on page 32!

Round the planets

Think of the 'halfway number' between the numbers. It will end in 5000.

Remember
Find the 'halfway number' between the nearest multiples – if the given number is less than the halfway number, then round down. If the given number is halfway or greater than the halfway number, then round up.

1 Write the two nearest multiples of 1000.
Circle the multiple of 1000 that the number rounds to.

a   86000   **86843**   (87000)   b _____   **44361** _____

c _____ **72450** _____   d _____ **90501** _____

2 Write the two nearest multiples of 10 000. Circle the multiple of 10000 that the number rounds to.

a (510000) **513938** 520000   b _____ **345799** _____

c _____ **844999** _____   d _____ **955000** _____

3 Write the two nearest multiples of 100 000. Circle the multiple of 100000 that the number rounds to.

a (400000) **483485** 500000   b _____ **747397** _____

c _____ **250000** _____   d _____ **849898** _____

4 Write the missing numbers in the table.

		Round to the nearest 1000	Round to the nearest 10000	Round to the nearest 100000
a	77 465			
b	834 808			
c	493 587			
d	949 139			

5 Round the diameters of the planets.

Remember

The rounded number is the lower multiple if the original number is less than the halfway number. The rounded number is the higher multiple if the original number is equal to or greater than the halfway number.

	VENUS	JUPITER	SATURN	URANUS
Diameter(km)	12 104	142 984	120 536	51 118
Rounded to the nearest 100 km				
Rounded to the nearest 1000 km				
Rounded to the nearest 10 000 km				
Rounded to the nearest 100 000 km				

Check

Check that you have rounded numbers under 5, 50, 500, 5000, 50 000, 500 000 down and those above are rounded up.

Well done!

Give yourself a sticker

Now – track how you're doing on page 32!

What's the problem?

1 Work out the 'secret' numbers using the clues provided.
Write the number as a numeral and in words.

 a

Clue 1: A 5-digit number. The highest place value is 3 less than the lowest place value.

Clue 2: The tens place value is equal to the thousands place value and 4 more than the hundreds place value.

Clue 3: The thousands place value is 7 and is 2 less than the ones place value.

 is the secret number.

It can be written in words as _____

_____ .

 b

Clue 1: A 6-digit number with a ones place value of 1 and a thousands digit greater than 5.

Clue 2: The tens place value is an even number and a different digit from all the other place values.

Clue 3: The ten thousands place value is the difference between the hundreds and ones place values.

Clue 4: The hundred thousands place value is greater than 4 and is the product of the thousand and hundreds place values.

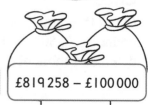 is the secret number.

It can be written in words as _____

_____ .

2 Compare the bank accounts using the symbols **<** or **>**.

a

£67 354 ☐ £66 245 + £1000 + 100 + £10

b

£92 989 ☐ £94 097 − £1000 − £100 − £10

c

£546 431 ☐ £445 421 + £100 000

d

£707 268 ☐ £819 258 − £100 000

Stickers for page 8

> > > > < < < <

Stickers for page 13

–4°C –5°C –6°C –7°C –8°C –9°C –10°C

–11°C –13°C –15°C –16°C –20°C –25°C

Stickers for page 28

11.05 a.m.	2.00 p.m.	12.00 p.m.
10.05 a.m.	2.40 p.m.	10.20 a.m.

Stickers for page 29

| 3:26 | 3:46 | 4:26 | 4:46 | 5:46 | 9:51 | 10:35 | 11:35 | 12:35 |

Character stickers

Reward stickers

3 This table gives estimates of bird populations in the UK.
Use the data to answer the questions.

Bird	Barn swallow	Yellow hammer	Herring gull	Redwing	Fieldfare	Mallard
Population estimate	752 723	713 327	731 070	709 237	713 702	709 372

a Write the populations in ascending order:

_____ < _____ < _____ < _____ < _____ < _____

b Write the populations in descending order:

_____ > _____ > _____ > _____ > _____ > _____

c Over a year, the population of Barn swallows decreases by 40 000 and the population of Yellowhammers and Redwings each increases by 10 000.

Write the new populations in ascending order:

_____ < _____ < _____ < _____ < _____ < _____

4 A scuba diver starts his journey from a height of 6 metres above sea level. What is his depth if he descends at the following rates? (The rate includes his descent on land.)

> The depths will all be negative numbers.

a 3 metres every 10 seconds for 40 seconds? ⬭ m

b 4 metres every 10 seconds for 50 seconds? ⬭ m

c 5 metres every 10 seconds for 60 seconds? ⬭ m

Check
You could draw a number line to check your answers to Question 4. ☐

Well done!

Give yourself a sticker

Now – track how you're doing on page 32!

Roman roads

1 Write the missing numerals in the tables.

> **Remember**
> Roman numerals only represent numbers that begin with the
> digits 1 or 5, e.g. 1 (I), 5 (V), 10 (X), 50 (L), 100 (C), 500 (D),
> 1000 (M). It's how you arrange them that gives other numbers.

Arabic numeral	Roman numeral
78	
	XCVI
109	
	CCLXXVII
353	

Arabic numeral	Roman numeral
	CDVIII
513	
	DCLXXXVI
849	
	CMXCIII

> The Romans built roads as straight as possible, in order to travel as quickly as they could!

2 Write the letter codes for the roads in the order given. The
length of the Roman roads is given in Roman numerals.

a

ROAD A	ROAD B	ROAD C	ROAD D	ROAD E
CCCXLIV metres	CCCLXXIV metres	CCCXLVII metres	CCXCIV metres	CCXLIX metres

Descending order: Road ( ) > Road ( ) > Road ( ) > Road ( ) > Road ( )

b

ROAD A	ROAD B	ROAD C	ROAD D	ROAD E
DCCLXXVII metres	DCCLXXXVII metres	DCCLXXVIII metres	DCCXCV metres	DCCLIX metres

Ascending order: Road ( ) > Road ( ) > Road ( ) > Road ( ) > Road ( )

3 Match the Roman numerals to the years when museum staff made models of the Roman roads.

Built by museum staff in

MCMXCIX

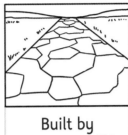
Built by museum staff in

MMVII

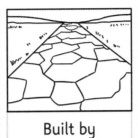
Built by museum staff in

MCMXCVII

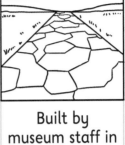
Built by museum staff in

MMXIV

Built by museum staff in

MMXVII

| 1997 | 2014 | 1999 | 2017 | 2007 |

4 Complete the missing numbers in the tables.

Year (Roman numerals)	Year (Arabic numerals)
	2004
MCMLXXIII	
	1547
MCCCLI	
	1299
MCLXVIII	
	1066
MXIX	
	999
CMLXXXIX	

Well done!

Give yourself a sticker

Now – track how you're doing on page 32!

Travel time

1 A family is travelling around the country in their car visiting friends. They make six journeys, one each day. Complete the line graph to show this data.

Day	Number of Miles
Monday	40
Tuesday	55
Wednesday	70
Thursday	80
Friday	65
Saturday	50

We still use the mile as a measure of distance on our roads in the UK.

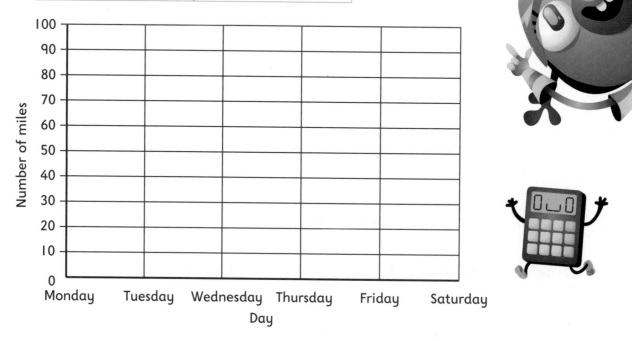

a How many more miles did the family travel on Wednesday than Tuesday?

_____

b How many fewer miles did the family travel on Saturday than Thursday?

_____

c Which two days show the biggest difference in miles covered?

_____

d How many miles is this difference?

_____

2 A boy is on a cycling trip. Every hour he makes a note of how far he has travelled away from home and uses this data to plot a graph.

Use the information in the graph to answer the questions.

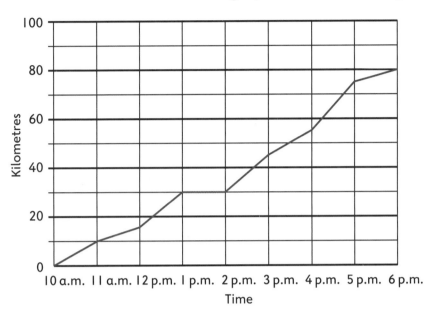

a How far was the boy from home at...

i 11 a.m.? _____ km

ii 2 p.m.? _____ km

iii 4 p.m.? _____ km

iv 6 p.m.? _____ km

b How many kilometres did the boy cycle between...

i 11 a.m. and 12 p.m.? _____ km

ii 2 p.m. and 3 p.m.? _____ km

iii 4 p.m. and 5 p.m.? _____ km

iv 12 p.m. and 4 p.m.? _____ km

c Between which pair of times (consecutive hours) did the boy travel...

... the greatest distance? _____ and _____

... the shortest distance? _____ and _____

d What do you think he was doing between 1 p.m. and 2 p.m.?

_____

Well done!

Give yourself a sticker

> **Check**
> Your graph readings need to be accurate. Use a ruler to check where points on the line cross the y-axis (vertical). ☐

Now – track how you're doing on page 32!

Temperature scales

1 The table below shows the water temperature as a beaker of water was heated up using a gas burner. Construct a line graph and use it to answer the questions that follow.

Remember
Correctly label your graph's axes and give it a title.

You will need to decide on a suitable scale for the y-axis: too small and not all of the data will fit in; too large and the line graph will be too small to read.

Time (minutes)	0	1	2	3	4	5	6	7	8
Temperature (°C)	15	20	30	45	55	65	75	85	90

Title: _____

a What is the temperature of the water at the following times…

1.5 minutes _____°C   3.5 minutes? _____°C   7.5 minutes? _____°C?

b By how many degrees did the temperature rise between the following times…

i 1 and 4 minutes _____ degrees

ii 2.5 and 4.5 minutes? _____ degrees?

iii 5.5 and 8 minutes _____ degrees

iv 0.5 and 7.5 minutes? _____ degrees?

c Between which pair of times (consecutive minutes) did the temperature increase the quickest?   _____ mins and _____ mins

Check
Make sure you have plotted all your graph points correctly. ☐

2 A class recorded the temperature outside their classroom throughout the year. They made a line graph displaying the data they collected.

Use the information in the graph to answer the questions.

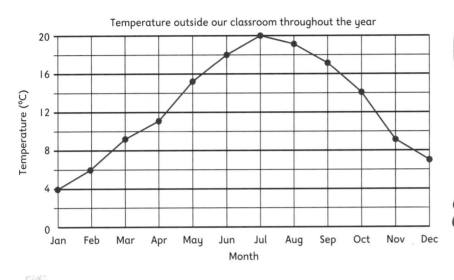

Temperature outside our classroom throughout the year

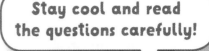

Stay cool and read the questions carefully!

There might be more than one for some of the answers.

a In which month was the temperature...

i 9°C _____

ii 15°C _____

iii 17°C _____

iv 7°C? _____

b Between which consecutive months was there a...

i rise of 4°C? _____ and _____

ii fall of 3°C? _____ and _____

iii rise of 3°C? _____ and _____

iv fall of 5°C? _____ and _____

c How much higher was the temperature in...

i June than January? _____ °C

ii May than December? _____ °C

iii September than February? _____ °C

iv April than November? _____ °C

Well done!

Give yourself a sticker

Now – track how you're doing on page 32!

Missing data

Remember
Both the table and the graph use exactly the same data.

The greatest rise or fall in data values is shown by the steepest lines on the graph.

1 The number of cupcakes sold each day in a bakery was recorded. The data was used to construct a line graph.

Unfortunately, some of the data in the table and the graph has gone missing. Use your data detective skills to complete the missing information and then draw the lines of the graph.

Day	Mon	Tue	Wed	Thu	Fri	Sat	Sun
Number of cakes sold		19		31		18	

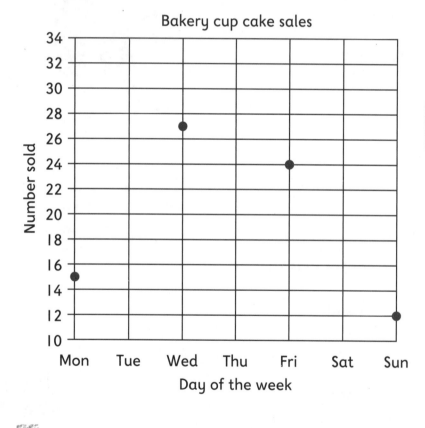

Bakery cup cake sales

Number sold / Day of the week

Don't forget to use a ruler to join the points on your graph.

a How many more cakes were sold on Tuesday than Sunday?

b How many fewer cakes were sold on Monday than Wednesday?

c Which consecutive days showed the greatest rise in cake sales?

_____ and _____

d Which consecutive days showed the greatest fall in cake sales?

_____ and _____

2 The number of people attending a music concert each evening was recorded. The data was used to construct a line graph.

Unfortunately, some of the data in the table and the graph has gone missing. Use your data detective skills to complete the missing information and then draw the lines of the graph.

Day	1	2	3	4	5	6	7	8	9	10
Number of people	150		350		700	450			950	500

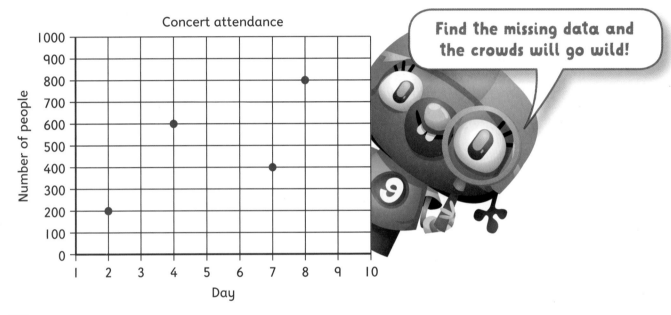

Concert attendance

Find the missing data and the crowds will go wild!

a How many more people attended the concert on day 5 than day 2? _____

b How many fewer people attended the concert on day 7 than day 9? _____

c Between which consecutive days showed the greatest rise in attendance?

_____ and _____

d Between which consecutive days showed the greatest fall in attendance? _____

and _____

Give yourself a sticker

Check
Make sure you compare the vertical (y-axis) values of points in neighbouring columns when answering 'consecutive days' questions. ☐

Now – track how you're doing on page 32!

Time for timetables!

1 Here is a timetable for a train journey from Moorland to Wetworth.

Remember
a.m. refers to times in the morning and p.m. refers to times in the afternoon or evening.

Moorland Departure	Wetworth Arrival
9.00 a.m.	10.00 a.m.
9.30 a.m.	10.30 a.m.
10.00 a.m.	11.00 a.m.
10.30 a.m.	11.30 a.m.
11.00 a.m.	12.00 a.m.
11.30 a.m.	12.30 p.m.
12.00 p.m.	1.00 p.m.

Use the timetable to answer the following questions.

a What time do I need to catch the train to be at Wetworth before 11.00 a.m.?

_____

b What time will I arrive at Wetworth if I leave Moorland at 11.30 a.m.?

_____

c How long does it take to travel between the two towns? _____

d If the 9.30 a.m. train from Moorland is delayed by 20 minutes, at what

time does it reach Wetworth? _____

e What time do I need to catch the train to be at Wetworth by 12.15 p.m.?

_____

2 A new timetable is produced that adds 25 minutes to each departure time and 35 minutes to each arrival time. Complete the new timetable below.

Moorland Departure	Wetworth Arrival
9.55 a.m.	
	11.35 a.m.
	12.35 a.m.
12.25 p.m.	

Timetables help a person know what is going to happen and when.

3 The bus timetable below shows all the stops between Shorthampton to Longham.

Use the information in the table to answer the questions below.

Shorthampton	9.10 a.m.	9.40 a.m.	10.05 a.m.	10.35 a.m.	11.10 a.m.	11.40 a.m.
Frosby	9.25 a.m.	9.55 a.m.	10.20 a.m.	10.50 a.m.	11.25 a.m.	11.55 a.m.
Cabmouth	9.42 a.m.	10.12 a.m.	10.37 a.m.	11.07 a.m.	11.42 a.m.	12.12 p.m.
Newtown	9.49 a.m.	10.19 a.m.	10.44 a.m.	11.14 a.m.	11.49 a.m.	12.19 p.m.
Midlington	10.07 a.m.	10.37 a.m.	11.02 a.m.	11.32 a.m.	12.07 p.m.	12.37 p.m.
Pottersby	10.22 a.m.	10.52 a.m.	11.17 a.m.	11.47 a.m.	12.22 p.m.	12.52 p.m.
Ringstone	10.42 a.m.	11.12 a.m.	11.37 a.m.	12.07 p.m.	12.42 p.m.	1.12 p.m.
Longham	11.06 a.m.	11.36 a.m.	12.01 p.m.	12.31 p.m.	1.06 p.m	1.36 p.m.

a If I catch the 10.12 a.m. train from Cabmouth, at what time will I reach Ringstone? _____

b If I catch the 11.25 a.m. train from Frosby, at what time will I reach Pottersby? _____

c How many minutes does it take to travel from...

i ... Newtown to Midlington? _____   **ii** ... Frosby to Cabmouth? _____

iii ... Ringstone to Longham? _____   **iv** ...Pottersby to Ringstone? _____

d Which two neighbouring stations are the shortest travel time apart?

_____ and _____

e Which two neighbouring stations are the longest travel time apart?

_____ and _____

f I want to get to Midlington by 11 a.m. What time is the latest train I can catch from Shorthampton? _____

g I want to get to Pottersby by 12.15 p.m. What time is the latest train I can catch from Frosby? _____

h I want to get to Longham by 1.30 p.m. What time is the latest train I can catch from Cabmouth _____

Give yourself a sticker

Check
Have you used the fact that there are 60 minutes in one hour? ☐

From start to finish

1 Complete the table by filling in the elapsed time.

Start time	End time	Elapsed time (hours and minutes)
7.30 a.m.	8.35 a.m.	1 hour and 5 minutes
8.15 a.m.	8.55 a.m.	
9.05 a.m.	10.15 a.m.	
10.25 a.m.	11.45 a.m.	
10.50 a.m.	12.50 p.m.	
12.20 p.m.	3.40 p.m.	
2.45 p.m.	7.55 p.m.	

2 Use these lesson durations to complete the following school timetable and then find the stickers with the correct times.

Lesson duration					
English	Maths	Science	P.E.	History	Art
55 minutes	50 minutes	1 hour and 5 minutes	1 hour and 15 minutes	45 minutes	40 minutes

Lesson	Start time	End time
Maths	9.30 a.m.	
Art	1.20 p.m.	
English	9.10 a.m.	
History	1.55 p.m.	
P.E.	9.50 a.m.	
Science	10.55 a.m.	

Don't miss the start of this lesson!

28

3 Complete the missing times in the table.

Flight from	Flight to	Flight time	Departure	Arrival
London	Glasgow	1 hour and 25 minutes	6.40 a.m.	
Manchester	Paris	1 hour and 50 minutes		9.45 a.m.
Dublin	Brussels		11.30 a.m.	1.35 p.m.
Cardiff	Madrid	4 hours and 10 minutes		5.05 p.m.
London	New York	6 hours and 55 minutes	4.50 p.m.	
Manchester	Moscow	5 hours and 40 minutes		4.25 a.m.
Birmingham	Cairo		11.50 p.m.	6.35 a.m.

4 Complete the start and finish times using the stickers provided.
You won't need them all!

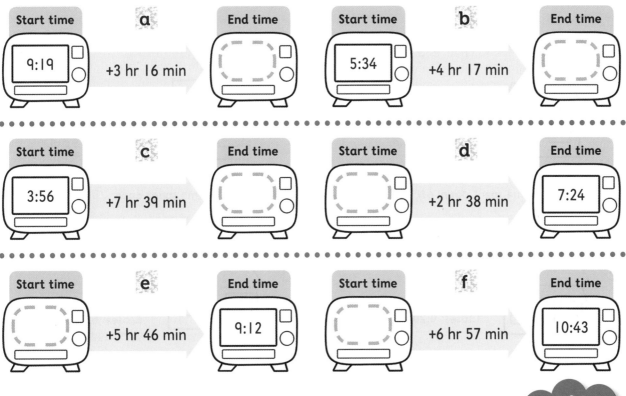

Check

Use a timeline to check your answers.

Well done!

Now – track how you're doing on page 32!

What's the problem 2?

1 Complete the Roman numeral additions.

Remember
Convert the numbers to Arabic numerals and then add them.

a LXXV + XVI = _____75_____ + _____16_____ = _____91_____

b LXVIII – XLIX = _____ – _____ = _____

c XLVI + LIII = _____ + _____ = _____

d LXXI – XLVI = _____ – _____ = _____

e LXXI + XI = _____ + _____ = _____

You can give your answer in arabic or Roman numerals!

2 Calculate the opening times of each shop.

a
Opens: _____ : _____
Closes: 4:30 p.m.
Time spent open: 6h 15m

b
Opens: _____ : _____
Closes: 5:15 p.m.
Time spent open: 7h 30m

c
Opens: _____ : _____
Closes: 9:20 p.m.
Time spent open: 10h 50m

d
Opens: _____ : _____
Closes: 6:25 p.m.
Time spent open: 8h 55m

e
Opens: _____ : _____
Closes: 8:20 p.m.
Time spent open: 13h 30m

f
Opens: _____ : _____
Closes: 3:05 p.m.
Time spent open: 9h 20m

3 Use the line graph to answer the questions.

A double line graph is used to compare two groups of related data over time.

Number of games won each year

Key
— Redbridge United
— Greyham City

Games won — 0, 5, 10, 15, 20, 25, 30, 35, 40, 45

2015 2016 2017 2018 2019

a How many more games did Greyham City win than Redbridge United in 2015?

b How many more games did Greyham City win than Redbridge United in 2019?

c Which two years saw the greatest difference in games won between the two teams?

_____ and _____

d Which two years saw the smallest difference in games won?

_____ and _____

e How many games in total did both teams win from 2015 to 2019?

f How many games in total did Greyham City win from 2015 to 2019?

g What is the difference in total games won between the two teams over these years?

Well done!

Give yourself a sticker

Check
Try using a timeline to check your answers.

Now – track how you're doing on page 32!

Progress Chart

Colour in a face.

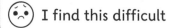

	I can do this well
	I can do this but need more practice
	I find this difficult

Page	I can . . .	How did you do?
2–3	I can write a number up to 6-digits as the sum of its place values.	😊 😐 😞
4–5	I can read and write numbers up to 1 000 000.	😊 😐 😞
6–7	I can work with numbers up to 1 000 000.	😊 😐 😞
8	I can compare numbers up to 1 000 000.	😊 😐 😞
9	I can order numbers up to 1 000 000.	😊 😐 😞
10–11	I can count forwards or backwards in steps of powers of 10.	😊 😐 😞
12–13	I can count forwards and backwards with positive and negative numbers, including through zero.	😊 😐 😞
14–15	I can round any number up to 1 000 000 to the nearest 10, 100, 1 000, 10 000 and 100 000.	😊 😐 😞
16–17	I can solve number problems working with numbers up to 1 000 000.	😊 😐 😞
18–19	I can read Roman numerals to 1000 (M) and recognise years written in Roman numerals.	😊 😐 😞
20–21	I can solve problems using information presented in a line graph.	😊 😐 😞
22–23	I can plot a line graph and solve problems using the information.	😊 😐 😞
24–25	I can find missing information and solve problems with data and a line graph.	😊 😐 😞
26–27	I can read and complete information in tables, including timetables.	😊 😐 😞
28–29	I can work with timetables and determine durations.	😊 😐 😞
30–31	I can solve problems involving Roman numerals and time intervals.	😊 😐 😞

How did you do?

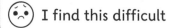